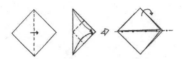

ORIGAMI DOVE

POETRY BY SUSAN MUSGRAVE

SUSAN MUSGRAVE

ORIGAMI DOVE

POEMS

McClelland & Stewart

LIBRARY AND ARCHIVES CANADA CATALOGUING IN PUBLICATION

Musgrave, Susan, 1951–
Origami dove / Susan Musgrave.

Poems.
ISBN 978-0-7710-6522-4

I. Title.

PS8576.U7O75 2011   C811'.54   C2010-905268-4

Library of Congress Control Number: 2010940061

We acknowledge the financial support of the Government of Canada through the Book Publishing Industry Development Program and that of the Government of Ontario through the Ontario Media Development Corporation's Ontario Book Initiative. We further acknowledge the support of the Canada Council for the Arts and the Ontario Arts Council for our publishing program.

Typeset in Seria by M&S, Toronto
Printed and bound in Canada

This book was produced using 100% recycled materials.

McClelland & Stewart Ltd.
75 Sherbourne Street
Toronto, Ontario
M5A 2P9
www.mcclelland.com

1 2 3 4 5   15 14 13 12 11

to Shabe Lohrasbe

who helps keep the birds of sadness from nesting in my hair

PART ONE

MADAGASCAR VANILLA

PART TWO

OBITUARY OF LIGHT: The Sangan River Meditations | 21

PART THREE

RANDOM ACTS OF POETRY

PART FOUR
HEROINES

ORIGAMI DOVE

PART ONE

MADAGASCAR VANILLA

Another Valentine's Day behind bars
and I bring you light from the stars
that you might find your way back to us
out of darkness. I bring you memories
of me – naked, happy, nine months' pregnant
tasting applesauce in the kitchen.

I bring you the wind, the way
our house creaked as you rocked
our newborn daughter who couldn't sleep.

I bring a handful of rain
that you may remember the sound of it,
and the smell of the earth
when you turn it in your hands.
I don't know why our life took
the turn it did, but now the smell
of earth reminds you – the magnolia
tree you planted the day
our daughter was born: did it live?

I bring you tears, the ones you wept
mixed with the milky scent of those I kept
locked up in me as we sang our daughter
to sleep those first merciful years –
if I could I would give you wings
to carry you up to the sky.

When I kiss your eyes, your sudden cry
startles the magnolia to a deeper white.

smelled of Madagascar vanilla.
After touching you for the last time
I scrubbed the scent from my skin – I would try
to remember later what the water felt like
on my hands but it was like trying to remember
thirst when you are drowning. They say love
doesn't take much, you just have to be there
when it comes around. I'd been there
from the beginning, I've been here all along.

I believed in everything: the hope
in you, your brokenness, the way
you arranged cut flowers on a tray
beside my blue-and-white teacup, the cracked
cup I'd told you brought me luck, the note
you wrote, *These flowers are a little ragged*
– like your husband. The day you died

of an overdose in Vancouver
I found a moonshell in the forest, far
from the sea; when I picked it up
and pressed it to my ear I could hear you
taking the last breath you had the sad luck

to breathe. Our daughter cupped her hands
over her ears, as if she could stop death
from entering the life she had believed in
up until now. Childhood as she had known it
was over: the slap
of the breakers, the wind bruising the sea

tells her she is no longer safe in this world –
it's you she needs. I see you pulling away
after shooting up in the car while we
stood crying on the road, begging
you to come home. The vast sky
does not stop wild clouds
from flying. This boundless grieving,
for whom is it carried on?

Nothing out of the ordinary, only
a doe and her fawn nudging
the hard yellow apple
you left on the grass, a fist-sized
Golden Delicious, the kind
that makes your mouth bleed
when you bite into it. The doe
raises her head when you step out
onto the deck to smoke your last
cigarette of the evening. Nothing
out of the ordinary, only the same
forgivable habit. I say, nothing
when you ask what's the matter
later, and then I start weeping
I can't help it I can't
stop.

and it's Anny's for eggs, a few
so big they won't fit in the carton she tries
her damnedest to squeeze them into. Some
are pale blue like the moon on those nights
I believe grief comes to me on wings:
who was it called hope *that feathered thing.*

If the barn's empty you might catch Anny
leading her grey horses home from the pasture,
a few scatty chickens nattering
at her feet. Last week she tossed
two roosters in her stockpot: rape
is one thing she won't tolerate in the barnyard.

Her black dog sighs when I arrive
and when I leave, Anny's eggs in the bursting
carton the perfect measure of sorrow, or so
I lead myself to believe.

sees everyone's future; it's his
business. He sees the one
with the beautiful neck that will
soon be broken by the other
with the sensitive hands sitting
next to her, sipping a Corona.
He sees the one who will come to him
in pieces, her body dismembered
by an estranged lover because,
as he confessed to the press,
she wouldn't give him any. The coroner
will be careful to note
the body has not been interfered with.

At night he comes to the taverna
to be alone, the sickness he has tasted
during the day consuming his thoughts
like beauty. And beauty is what he seeks
though how you know beauty when you see it
is the question he asks each time he cuts
open a young body and finds something
beautiful but malignant inside. There are
things he won't discuss with anyone,
even the boys who bring him illicit
pleasures, boys he can be
himself with again, when the knife's rinsed.

In the taverna he does not have to think
what will become of these boys once beauty
has outgrown them and they have turned

into uncertain men. He does not have to see
the one who lies before him on the slab,
a long way from home and the pleasures
they shared, the drugs, the cigarettes, his
grotesque lungs now squeezing upwards
into his collarbones, to suck their last
small breath. At the taverna
he does not have to see the track marks
on the boy's skinny arm sticking out
from under him on the bed. The coroner
can sometimes forget the boy's grace, the way
he kneeled to kiss those forbidden places: nothing
touches him here, not even love.

On the other side of the river the wild
cattle graze – I think, nothing is strange
to me – a heaviness has gone.

My hands smell of horses. Last night
riding along the riverbank in a dream,
I felt a bullet graze me; riding a stray horse
across frozen sand on the far side of the river
I could feel what might have been my own death
pass me by. Maybe this lightness now

has to do with the dream, or simply
the heart's resolve to keep beating on
in a place of darkness; don't we stop
grief from cutting deeper, sometimes,
with our tears? Years ago a poet who became
my first great love wrote, *there are no*
blue stones. Ever since I have searched
for one, as if to prove him wrong – what,
if anything, have I learned? The poet
had been a prisoner when he was young, a man
who still believes there are some ideals
worth dying for. They kept him in a box
no bigger than a poor man's coffin,
in a room they called the dark place,
la oscura. What saved him, he said,
was a belief in what persists, the faith
he still keeps, that tenderness exists.

Nothing is *strange to me*. Today I rode
over frozen snow to the dunes
and found, on the other side of the river,
a stone deeper than any blue I'd known –
deeper than my first love's eyes the night
I watched him kissing someone new. I wonder
if, in his sick-bed on the other side
of the Atlantic, he felt me cry
and touch the blue stone to my lips?
It wasn't meant to be
that kind of kiss.

ALL THE WILD WINDS OF THE WORLD
GO HOWLING THROUGH YOU

as you write one more poem of longing
and send it shivering into the next world
because, inside you, it no longer has a home.

What do you expect –
to sit under the cedar trees
all day and come away the wiser?

Your boy on the winter beach knee-deep in foam,
laughing and stumbling towards his father's arms,
like the rest of us, perhaps, longing for home.

Every Christmas Eve we would drive
through the ritzy district to see
the coloured lights my father said
were an utter waste of electricity.
He took the long way home, the way
that wound away around the orphanage –
a waste of gas, my mother thought,
but for once didn't say – and I would
imagine, for an instant, a world
where someone is grateful for something.
As we slowed past that desperate house
always in darkness, those poor bastards,
my father would say. The pitch of their roof
made it impossible for Santa's reindeer
to land there. At home we'd hang stockings,
leave milk and shortbread by the chimney,
whisper our prayers, and I'd lie awake thinking
what it must feel like to have no one.
Every year my father took the one
trustworthy ladder we owned and climbed high
onto our flat roof and sat drinking
whiskey and ringing bells so we would go on
being deceived as long as it was possible
to go on being children; he knew love
and treachery were part of the same

bargain. Lately I have come to believe
all that is of value is the currency
of the heart, so that when my father
lay dying, I forgave God. I had never believed

in him until then, but found myself
forgiving him for the space he had never filled,
the loneliness in me he had created. Now I know:
between birth and death there is only
loneliness, so big sometimes it makes love
seem spectacularly small, with no grave
big enough to contain our grief. Loneliness

takes the good out of all of our goodbyes,
more permanent than the sadness you know
when your lover drives away having lost
interest in everything about you, especially
your suffering. Love's a blip, a glitch,
but loneliness signs on for the duration,
one gunshot wound to the head is all it takes
to assure your allotted space in today's
News of the World beside the Bangladeshi woman
caned 101 times for having an abortion, misery
being careless and everywhere
at the same time. Loneliness is so big

that when it moves into your house you feel
as if someone has moved away, warmed up the Dead
Wagon with one headlight missing
and made for the highway still chasing
love, the thing you both swore you'd always die for.
Now loneliness has laid me instead, lopsided,
on the table, so that when they come to view me,
the one or two people who tried to know me will say,
She never looked that way, he's got her mouth
all wrong, as if the living shouldn't have to see
how right we finally become. If my mouth looks wrong

it's because I am trying to find the way
to tell you I have become the AIDS baby
who doesn't want to die until she has seen
her first snow, an origami dove
chased by a flying child under a snow-dusted
schoolbus in Ontario, now buried
a kindly stone's throw from a frozen river.
The cure for loneliness, they say, is solitude,
trust everybody but cut the cards, take your delight
in momentariness, avoid adjectives of scale,
you will love the world more and desire it
less: all sound advice. There are 101 words
for freedom, not one from the kind of pain
the woman must have suffered after 101
lashes with a cane, cut, I suspect,
specifically for one purpose. Sex, death,
our fragile lives are like the knife edge
of the wind scraping away the sky. I see how true
loneliness has become when he takes up with me
and walks me through the world I have always
called my home. Only in darkness I see now
it has never been my home.

TRUE LOVE

> No remembering, no forgetting:
> The secret of true love.
> – Zen saying

As if you were to fill
a shapeless bowl with stars
and wash clouds in it until
your sorrow begins to drift away
from this world of remembering,
and the forgetting. As if you were

to hear the teardrops of the smallest
insects falling on the leaves of the crucifix
lilies along the riverbank: you know
everything is weeping, so why
when you weep you think you are alone?

Listen to the voiceless words,
the shore giving thanks for the sea.
I went with my grief but when I reached
the rivermouth the ocean said,
take me, instead, take me.

As if this robe of mist I wear
makes me any more noble
or more humble than the smoke
from your campfires, laughter
rivering the heart. Who is beloved, who
in the wind? As if the shape

of this bowl can be round in one moment,
square the next. The grass still bends
the way the wind goes.

The ravens arrived before daybreak,
awakening me. I moved from my moonlit
bed to the window, my heartbeat the sound
a hammer makes striking emptiness, before
and after. How much easier to embrace
pain than the common miracles of freezing
rain, the fires of smudgy juniper
smouldering across the water,
or the mist that stills its whispery music
in my mind. What sound does the wind make
if you don't name it? Oh my ancestors
you are like clouds with nothing
to keep you from flying, like the running-away
river with no one to depend on. I go outside
understanding the sky is
just as present beneath my feet as it is
up above, and so try to tread
lightly on the crust of this earth, knowing
it is thin. The ravens slope towards the stars,
the black night in their beaks, and I think,
be light, light, light, as I make my way
in darkness to the river's edge. And then,
from overhead, a branch drooping
with snow, the owl takes flight, swoops
and glides down beside me. Even though
the requiem birds had failed to roust him
from his place of refuge, it is my quiet
uneasiness that causes him to strike
out over the river, to the brighter side.
What brings tears, I do not know, nor grasp

the thief-like tendency of tears to disappear,
but I feel graced to have felt the snow
owl's breath upon my face, as if I no longer need
to go on breathing; I am being breathed.
Be light, I whisper to the wind
as I climb the bank back to my dreaming
bed, nodding at the green bamboo stalk
I used to stake an unruly chrysanthemum
clinging to life in the frozen garden. The going
doesn't get any easier, but by any name
I'd miss the wind too much to be
parted from this life for even one hard winter.

PART TWO

OBITUARY OF LIGHT

The Sangan River Meditations

Winter

(i)

After the first snowfall I find
a winter wren frozen on the forest path.

Who could have imagined it?
Even the birds are freezing!

As I push through earth locked in sorrow,
in ice, find a hollow between rocks
where her body will lie, a winter wren lights
on the handle of my shovel.

(ii)

Across the river, children
are eating snow, their lips
the colour of tiny kingfishers
in the numbing cold. The delight
they take in the melting of each
snowflake on their tongues reminds me:
joy is there, in everything, and even
when we can't see it.

(iii)

So many times Paul has explained
how a southwest wind ninety miles
off shore creates a ground swell
that blows the scallops in on North Beach
but only if there's a northwesterly
and particularly after a southeaster.
So many times: how can I not remember?

(iv)

Snowflakes melt on my face,
a lifetime passes away.
The deep muttering of rocks
in the black river. Why am I
ill at ease?

(v)

A wild swan served on a bed
of her whitest feathers, the dusty
flavour of potatoes steeped in cream.
I poured wine chilled in the river
since this afternoon when the first
black clouds rolled up on the horizon.
When the cat came in licking the snow
from her paws, our guests dropped
their eyelids in pleasure.
All evening I had been promising snow.
One of them quoted poetry.

(vi)

The stillness between tides and winds.
Snow blows through the emptiness
where my thoughts have been.

(vii)

The stars stab with their cold.
The day we are born we begin
to forget everything we know.

How then do we prepare
the body for its future? Already
my old eyes could see past
those stars if that is what I wished.
I see no further than this: a tree
weighted with snow. But when
the snow falls I think of it as my own.
That way it is lighter.

(viii)

As long as I am alive there will be
a snow of mist on the mirror.

In no time at all, I am home.

Spring

What I most want is to spring out of this personality,
then to sit apart from that leaping.
I've lived too long where I can be reached.
– Rumi, "Unseen Rain"

(i)

In another life, this place was my home.
I feel the rising of a forgotten knowledge
like a spring from hidden aquifers under the earth.

To glimpse your own nature is to come home
like the rainfall that turns to mist before touching the earth
then rises once again to praise the sky.

(ii)

A young eagle lights
on a gravel bar. How effortlessly
the rain drips from the eaves.

(iii)

A moment ago I heard
a raven speak: *feed me,*
stay away, come over here,
pay attention! Imagine! Up
until that moment the ravens
and I had not been on speaking terms.

(iv)

I wash lettuce in the river
separating the leaves to make sure
no dirt clings to the unearthed root.

Later, a simple meal of alder-smoked
salmon, and hard bread I baked over
a week ago. Later still I return to the river
with empty hands.

(v)

From the bridge I watch
the pure moving of the bird
over the bank where two children
pick the blue lupines I planted
that have since grown wild. I see
the raptor swoop, then change
his mind and disappear, think
how boundless is the pure
wind circling our lives.

(vi)

Paul's home from the hospital:
who would've guessed he could beat
lung cancer! Already he's up
making deals, vying to buy
my old Toyota for parts when I've
driven her into the ground.

(vii)

At low tide he would take me
to the places no one knew; he knew
I loved those blue-violet mussel shells,
their hairlike bonds. Driving home
along the beach I turned once
at White Creek to see a wisp
of white cloud spiralling into the sky
over the dome of Tow Hill,
just as if, I remember feeling,
a spirit were leaving a body.

(viii)

Our cat is up the tree again; I hear her cry
over the lonely tattering of prayer flags
worn to transparency by the wind. I try
tempting her down with heart minced the way
she likes it, still warm from the gutted
body of the deer. I build a bridge
from our roof to the end of her branch
so she can pad across and I can rescue her.

But no, it's as if she clings to the high
dying hemlock because she has
something she wants me to see.
Later, with the moon rising I climb back
onto our roof with my flashlight, her eyes
two shiny plum pits summoning me. She
is happy now that I have come just to sit
patiently and watch from this height
the river empty into the sea.

(ix)

Perhaps this is all
I have left to do

bow to the plum blossoms
in all those ancient love poems

loosely translated from the Chinese.

Summary

I have always known that at last I would take this road
But yesterday I did not know
it would be today.
– Narihara

(i)

Sun falling on yellow cedar
and my daughter in broken sandals
climbing the steps to her father's house.

(ii)

Taking a deep drink
of the river's ancient
darkness, you whisper,
kiss me, but my lips
aren't wet enough yet.

(iii)

Suffering is the way
we measure love, you say,
how much we have lost, how much
has been taken from us.

I keep looking out my window
as if there is anywhere left to go.

(iv)

I save your letter for last,
slice it open with the knife
you said was never sharp
enough. A broken heart
is an open heart. I hold the pieces
of your letter in my hand.

(v)

Soon you, too, will lose
all interest in your past.
Who is it you are
unable to forgive?
You're gone now and I
can't explain my faithful
longing for you.

(vi)

How empty the white bowl
by the back door waiting to be
filled, lonely the cracked
rubber ball, sad the comforter
abandoned on the grass. Fetch,
death said, and they left to chase
the wind: three good dogs,
Bubba, Nike, and Slu'gu.

(vii)

A young girl pulls herself along
like a broken cricket, her face
surrounded by pale sunlight
like Jesus. In a magazine

I find at the laundromat I read,
"We travel to faraway places to watch
in fascination the kind of people
we ignore at home." In the margin
someone has written, "Why do we do this."

(viii)

The moon-coloured stones
you piled high above the tide line –
in the morning they are still there!
Even the river stealing past
in the darkest night becomes another way
for grace to slip through.

(ix)

Stones bicker. Trees have bad days.
The brightest stars are not always
in the mood to sing. Pain
is simply there, like bread rising,
like driftwood, and sun in the garden
window. There is no place
to take shelter
but yourself.

(x)

Out of nowhere a low-flying
plane. I cover my ears
as a duck flaps up from the river,
squawking. I can still hear
the drone long after the plane
disappears. A duck's cry
doesn't echo, and no one knows why.

(xi)

I light a handful of leaves to make tea.
To fluff up my pillow I pull down an armload
of clouds. I've kept the same question
to myself for a thousand years.

When life stops, does death stop, too?

(xii)

There's just enough light left
on the river tonight to turn
the water black. You see it flare up
behind my eyes: the obituary of light.

Fall

*Sometimes I go about in pity for myself, and all the while
a great wind is bearing me across the sky.*
— Anishinaabe Ojibwe saying

(i)

The first alder leaves on the road after
last night's wind, those still clinging
to the trees blowing silver. If you ask me
again what I want it is to make
peace with the part of me that insists
I exist, like the scratching of our old cat
at the back door when the north wind blows.

(ii)

Small flocks of twitchy sandpipers
scoot out on the tide; a pheasant
stutters from the ditch into the trees.
All my life, right and wrong
tangled. A falcon stoops
in a steep glide.

(iii)

Wet leaves on the road,
the last foxgloves bowing their heads
to no one. Every act of pity
is a form of prayer. Our daughter
wants to know – do flowers hurt
when you cut them?

(iv)

Our daughter calls for you
to climb with her, the last leaves
yellow in the skeletal tree.
You'll find a way, she knows,
to make those gold apples rain.

(v)

One night's wind is enough
to strip the trees. Years ago
I strung prayer flags between
two dying hemlocks. Is it the flags
that flutter now, or the wind?

(vi)

I didn't even begin to know
loneliness until the fog bank
rolled in from Tow Hill all the way
to the Chown and stayed there
for days swallowing the world
I thought I'd come home to
in all its white silence.

(vii)

Out of the fog a herd of wild
cattle, two heifers locking horns
on the road while I try to steer the truck
around them without getting involved.
I thought I knew where I was going
when I set out, but now
I'm not so sure.

(viii)

We eluded beauty and went
right to the truth, evaded happiness
and went for the weeping. I loved you
with the fierceness we save for those
who can break us in all the broken places.
Never mind the lies, the promises
you couldn't keep. They are small
mysteries, like the blowing milkweed silk.

(ix)

Scraps of mist tumble on a bed
of wind. I dip my hands in the river,
cup water to my face, and drink
the evening in. At this moment I expect
nothing, but it wasn't always so.
Moments ago I feared the mist
would pass me over on my bed of stones.

(x)

The cries of the wild geese
sadden my heart. I am homesick
for when I was real. The wind blows
though my clothes as I stand by the open
window counting stars burning out, one
by one, in the darkness. How hard
they must have struggled to bring us
their dying light.

(xi)

He winds through pineapple grass
and salmon-coloured yarrow, one eye
on the black horizon: there's a big storm
blowing in and he's determined to beat it
home. I know this will be Paul's last
trip to the Spit. His brother who has come
from Nova Scotia squeezes his hand
and asks if he's ready
for more morphine. Pain has never stopped
Paul so I'm not surprised when I see
his shadow split off from the rest
of his body and slip back to face the storm
alone, his last cigarette flaring before
the wind extinguishes it.

(xii)

Yesterday Paul and I shared
an eggroll at the Golden Pam;
it took all he had left to draw
a map on his table napkin, the walks
he wanted me to take, up the Sangan
Ridge, down along the Skonun. There were
trees in there, he said, that were some kind

of beautiful. Only he said beauty-full,
as if beauty, too, had grown frail
and needed a rush of new
life breathed into it. We all knew Paul
was going to die; I just didn't think
it would be today.

    – September 7, 2005

(xiii)

Somedays just listening to him
breathe would be enough to suck
the breath out of sorrow. We all knew
he wasn't ready to accept
the earth's dark proposal, but he
accepted it.

(xiv)

The day we set out to dig
my old cat's grave under the looming
hoary cedars, the dark came down
earlier, blowing rain clouds
over the hills. I thought, *the going
doesn't get any easier.* We are the broken
heart of this world.

PART THREE

RANDOM ACTS OF POETRY

but, hey, listen up, nothing lasts.
They put me in a body bag when my bandages
came off, zipped me up quick and sent me
home to somebody else's life. I know

what I know. Your letters from death row
say you are making a comeback, my killer-cool
love and a lifelong dependency
on hallucinogens got you through,
and Hallelujah you've found
Jesus, too. I'm just about done like some
lonesome dog's dinner when I come to with this
smoking gun down the back of my throat
and a personage of great magnitude,
like God with a world view, comes creeping
into my room saying, *open your mouth and close
your eyes today or next week everyone you know
is going to die.* Turns out he was acting

on false information. My body was no weapon
of mass destruction, only a self-destructive mass
with gumdrop nipples and hardcore angel eyes.
Sometimes when I feel righteous I check out
into a Holiday Inn, take time off from my own
life to smoke crack or whatever designated
drug is currently discombobulating
the minds of the glued to-their-TVs

in-terror-populace this season. I was happy,
once, but God is pushing the deadlier

weapons these days, not even a snowflake
lands on my eyelids anymore without leaving
a bruise. Your last letter began *I'd die*
for you, and because that sounded promising
I made the mistake of reading through
to the inevitable end. *Did you ever*
receive that money order I was supposed to
send? I need it back. ASAP. Love don't
suck dead dog dick, pistol. Love supposed
to kick ass, way Jesus do.

Last night you dreamed I drove off
with a philosophical taxi-driver;
this time you knew I was leaving you
for good. In your dreams I betray you
every chance I get: why can't you dream
I stay with you just for once? *Those who do
not wish to kill anyone, wish they were able,*
wrote some long-ago Roman, observing
the darker side of human nature. In your dream

I am wearing ice-age lingerie, oblivious
to the effects of global warming. My bra
began to thaw as we entered Central Park
in that hot yellow cab with matching airbags –
my driver being for the future – while suddenly
in the back I became so much older,
like one of those people who like to get
to the airport early, and my panties melted
into a pool at my feet, where, centuries later,
archeologists would uncover the intimate remains
of a woman who once tore up Sixth Avenue
tossing away her constricting underthings.

In your dream you felt excluded
because I kept driving around all night
while you had your mind set
on finding a parking meter. Could this mean
we were incompatible, you said, as my driver
began to resemble Harvey Keitel starring
in *Bad Lieutenant* and he was

just like in the movie with his
philosophy of life: you can take the girl
out of the cheap underwear
but you can't take the cheap underwear
out of the girl. I said I would forgo
a receipt if he would shut off his meter
and join me in the back; I probably do have
a spiritual nature but in the backseat I can be
wholly animal. As your dream ended I was naked
in Critical Care, with Harvey in the same bed,
smoking. A sign above my life support system read,
Visitors to the dying must use the pay phone
at the end of the hall where the smoking room
used to be, but you didn't have the nerve
to ask Harvey to butt out because
he was for the future, which is where
you woke up, in Pathology between Shipping
and Receiving, where nothing I could do
would be enough to make you warm. Everything
in your life came together so perfectly
at that moment it would forever be
tinged with grief. Two days later I made up my mind
to lose weight without ever gaining it back again
on an ice-cream diet and you were arrested
for armed robbery. Toodle-oo.
Those were Harvey K's last words to me
on his death-bed, too. Toodle-oo.

AL PURDY TOOK A BUS
TO THE TOWN WHERE HERODOTUS WAS BORN

"The town we visited," Al says, "remember
the town – we caught a bus there."
Eurithe can't remember the name of the place
either, but she recalls a wake-up call
and a foreign voice saying, "Your cold breakfast
is coming up." The last time I made Al
a birthday cake it fell, but Al was gracious
enough to say, *thank you for your largesse.*

There are vast areas of my ————
that are missing, for instance the name
of the restaurant in Dublin where each dish
was an approximation of its ideal,
or the Christian names of my daughter's
schoolbus drivers I said I'd never forget:
Mrs. Blood, Mr. Wolf, and Miss Hood.
I wanted to write a Young Adult book
about "the late bus," the one the bad kids
always took, but I didn't want my obituary
ending up in the Entertainment Section
of the newspaper where I once found a prognosis
of Elizabeth Taylor's tumour. I don't want
to be anybody's Smile of the Day
which is why I'm glad I didn't shoot myself
cleaning Henry White's house on Haida Gwaii
last summer – my death would have made
the National Enquirer along with Wife Used
Cheating Hubby's Toothbrush to Clean the Commode.
In Henry White's house I sucked up a .22 bullet,

heard a bang, saw sparks, and the next thing
I remember I was seeing headlines: Woman Shoots Self
in Head with Vacuum Cleaner. The photograph
of my sad brain looks like a honeydew melon
soaked in V8 Juice all night after being run over
by a train the time I went pub-hopping in Oxford
and landed in a punk bar eating drugged cookies
which I worried about later when I started
hallucinating because I was pregnant
with Charlotte and didn't want her to be born
in the corridor of British Rail while I peaked
on Peek Frean digestive biscuits. Mary Oliver
says poems are ropes let down to the lost, I wish
someone would keep that in mind when they ever
find me. A critic in the *Globe* asks why
poets are always losing things, especially
people, why can't they *find* something
instead, and I believe he deserves an answer.

"The town where they lost your suitcase," Al says,
"remember the town – we caught a bus there."
Eurithe can't remember if her luggage showed up
but she does recall a wake-up call, a foreign
voice saying, "Your hour has come," and the line
going dead. You cherish people
then they are gone: what more can be said
about the ones I'd rather be with,
the ones I love best.

I thank them for their largesse.

PICK YOUR RUT CAREFULLY, YOU WILL BE IN IT
FOR THE NEXT 80 MILES, warned a sign on a stretch
of bad road near Head-Smashed-in Buffalo Jump,
Alberta. I love my country because even though
we have been called the vichyssoise of nations –
cold, half French, and difficult to stir – we are
honestly everything we pretend to be: one nation
of eighty ethnic groups who still base
our fashion taste on what doesn't itch.
If the United States is like the guy at the party
who gives everyone cocaine and still can't get
anybody to like him, north of the 49th parallel
where all our Christmases are white, Canadians
are the life of the party. God gave us memories
so we could have roses in winter, they say
in Manitoba, but on Vancouver Island we know
the cold of a Canadian winter can kill
even a memory. *Gather ye rosebuds*
was my old father's best advice.

The average Canadian considers life too short
to stuff a mushroom, thinks *poutine* is French
cuisine, is too polite to take the last
piece of Christmas cake from the plate,
the last perogy from the pot; the average
Canadian says *I'm sorry* 4.8 times a minute.
We are a self-effacing nation, a well-mannered lot:
Americans say no to drugs; Canadians say
no thank you. We are not elitists, says our new
Governor General: ask anyone who matters.

Canadians are unarmed Americans with health
care; a sign on the door of the Ontario
Legislature reads, WARNING TO ALL PERSONNEL:
FIRINGS WILL CONTINUE UNTIL MORALE IMPROVES.
Redd Foxx said health nuts are going to feel stupid someday,
lying in hospital dying of nothing,
but the unarmed, in Canada, will be covered.
If I had my life to live over
I'd live over HaidaBucks in Masset
on Haida Gwaii, order skim-milk latte
made from organic shade-grown beans only.
Whenever I felt lonely I'd drive down
to Margaret's Cafe in Queen Charlotte City
where a sign immemorial says, TOMORROW
HAS BEEN CANCELLED DUE TO LACK OF INTEREST.
I'd order spaghetti to go: what person on this
planet can feel lonely while eating
spaghetti? My new philosophy for the millennium:
dread one day at a time. Wake up
on New Year's Day and smell what's left
of the roses. Pick your rut carefully
but remember, better to be behind
a police car than in front of one. When you die
there is going to be a big vacuum in your life
so make hay while the sun still shines
through the ozone layer. Raise a glass
to the future, taste the stars.

   – December 31, 1999

What I want to say to His Honour
who sentenced the father of my children
to eighteen years for armed robbery
is let's just let bygones be bygones
be bye bye bye he'll be gone so long
but it doesn't come out that way, instead I say,
it's not like he knocked off a Food Bank,
Your Honour; nobody's going to bed hungry.
The first time this parole officer
comes to my house to see if I'm the kind
of woman suitable to be visiting her better half
in the bucket, he won't shake hands due to it
being flu season, a titch touchy. Your Honour,
having a parole officer in your house
is like going through airport security
without leaving home, jokes bomb
as mightily as the U.S. Forces
in Afghanistan. Last week leaving Deer Lake,
Newfoundland, the security guards
made me gulp down my bottled
Evian water to prove it wasn't a controlled
substance, my fault for pointing out
Evian is Naive spelled backwards: like the sign
says, joking is a criminal offence punishable
by whatever it takes to make a person think
twice before being a comedian. This encourages me,
I say, heard any good jokes lately to the comedian
in front of me who looks seriously like the dead
poet Al Pittman, and he cracks to me it is taking
so long to get through security he is afraid

his forged passport is going to expire
after which the drug-and-bomb-squad pit bulls
are onto him, taking formidable bites
out of his right to remain
silent; Al confesses he returned from the dead
without remembering to warn anyone
and is flying back to Kandahar under the alias
bin Pittman, which is why he wears the T-shirt
with the many faces of bin Laden on it
inside out. I try to diffuse the situation,
saying Al joined Al-Qaeda and all he got
was this lousy T-shirt but then when
it is my turn to be interrogated I err
on the side of terror and swallow the one bag
I haven't packed myself, a small bag
of white powder a criminal
lawyer in St. John's has given me
as a going-away gift. The false-sense-of-security
guards start sniffing around, and suddenly
I feel a new solidarity with Al
going away for good
to the jug in Corner Brook
so I get all Joan Baezy pro-active singing, "Ban
the bomb bomb bomb" he'll be gone so long
until I cough up the gift bag of white powder
a sodden bath bomb with Souvenir of The Rock
written on it for the love of Allah, so arrest me
why don't you, these are desperate times.
If you want my opinion they should detain
all passengers who don't board the aircraft joking:
a sense of humour should be a prerequisite
for anyone flying Air Canada these days.
Your Honour, when I offer this parole officer

coffee, he says I don't use caffeine
as if I've just suggested we inject heroin
with a turkey baster. Then he goes, *you ever
considered therapy?* like I must be
some kind of case to stand by a man who steals
honest money from an ATM to make ends meet.
I don't miss a beat. I spent twenty years
in analysis until my therapist finally said
three words that would forever change
my life, he said, *no hablo ingles.*
An old joke, Your Honour, but a good one,
ever notice when you cut *therapist*
in two you get *the* and *rapist*, how half of *anal-
ysis* is *anal?* When you analyze it that way
I don't need some bad-ass parole officer
repeating how my better half is bad, badder,
and baddest, why couldn't he try putting
my kids' dad in some kind of positive .
historical context? I mean, he ain't bad like
Hitler was bad, not like Stalin-bad,
Attila-the-Hun-bad, Jack-the-Ripper- or
George-the-Bush-bad, not half as bad
as the Baader Meinhof Gang. Furthermore I say
to him, when was the last time you went into
a bank feeling holy? That's when this excuse
for a parole officer pulls out his Corrections
Services Canada pen and writes that I am a minimizer
of my spousal equivalent's crimes, unsuited to visit
said spousal equivalent due to my non-deferential
attitude and negative influencing factors.
Your Honour, I had three words to say to said
parole officer after that:
no hablo ingles.

"Robbins Parking has assigned your unpaid Provincial
Offences fine(s) to our company for immediate collection."

Inside the house this enforcer
from the collection agency informs me
he's not here to waste any more of his life, picks
his teeth with the bamboo
splinter he threatens to stick through
my liver to avoid further collection activity
if I don't fork over; I tell him I have nothing
unless a beer can collection is considered
worldly goods. I've been through this
before, the door kicked in, the dog
left for dead in the driveway, the stereo playing
"This Is the End," stuck in the same spot
where I dropped acid on it in 1974. My daughter
who was named after a hurricane in the Minor
Antilles where I believe she was conceived
says buddy better leave before she gets her wind
up and does some major damage. She eats
these all-dressed chips, then goes
through a major personality change.
These days I'm running around
with a chicken like my head cut off
trying to get on with my childhood, or at least
over it. At late Dad's funeral my aggrieved mother
climbed onto the church roof and started shouting,
Your Father Who Art in Hell and though I thought
she was asserting herself finally it wasn't
the right moment. Later, stuck in a ditch
crying for my loss, a van pulled over and a woman

60
—

with two black eyes and a few teeth too many
missing asked was she on the right road
to Stormin' Norman's Paintball Adventures?
Isn't this the way life always goes? Life goes
on, I mean, you wish it would stop, if only
for a moment, so you could pause to apply
another layer of CoverGirl hydrating concealer
to soften the permanent lines of sorrow. One breath

mint at a time, I tell myself, as if anyone
on this lonely planet will be here to kiss me
goodbye or perform mouth to mouth on me
when I decide to give up breathing forever.
Every blade of grass has its angel that bends over it
and whispers, grow, grow, I say to this bad attitude
who has come all the way from Ontario to collect
for a parking ticket I couldn't take seriously
enough to pay. What do you do on your days
off, I say, lure families into bushes on ski slopes
and kill them?

How does he expect me to behave when some hired power
sticks a warning under my broken windshield wiper:
"Meter Indicates there is no time left"? I seriously stopped
buying green bananas for the rest of that week.
Now I'm busted, can't even afford the dog
a decent burial, stop with the condolences to Rover,
he hasn't rolled over since last week when the posse
comitatus broke in to repossess the furniture. Who needs

a front door anyway when there's no way out?
Who needs a love seat with a broken arm, or a bed
with no give? When I picture my body
these days, it's going for broke in a hot-wired hearse,

all these secondary veins and main arteries like
interconnecting highways full of unhappy accidents
waiting to happen. That's luck. I'm at this mall
watching the lifesized clock go tick tock tick
waiting for Hurricane Virginie to blow a hole
in my GST rebate, sacrificing my enjoyment for her
enjoyment, casing the joint wondering how desperate
a person would have to be to steal a faux crystal
lighted pineapple table centrepiece from the display
window of the Lite Up Your Life Interior Design store
when this masked gunman waving a To-Do list in my face
says to me, "Dude, look at the faux pineapple, dude,
look look it's expensive, dude, it's very fucking,
very very expensive"; what's the underworld coming to
where fake isn't even fake anymore, it's *faux*?
If you plan on taking down the Lite Up Your Life store,
I tell him, they don't take hold-up notes anymore unless
they've been notarized. The dog, the one you drove

over, his name's not Rover, we called him Zero
because, as my daughter goes, what's in a name?
Assets? *Dude.* Usual occupation? Put down
Hair Magnet inventor, patent pending. Put down
Girdles Toilet Seats with Sanitary Strips
on a volunteer basis. Don't write self-employed
grave-digger or how long it took me to dig self's
grave with used toothpick, don't put *snow underfoot*
goes crunch crunch crunch when I run around
outside with a chicken like my head cut off – you heard me
right the first time – just do what they pay you to do,
and the slate's wiped clean. Right now my blood tastes
sweeter than it's ever been – and there's lots of it – like
money you've never seen.

The day I won the Nobel Prize
for Peace, my mother was arrested
for stalking Knowlton Nash. The day
I woke up to find there were no drugs
in the house was the day I stopped coping
with reality. When I took up reading
contemporary poetry of bereavement I changed
my mind about being happy I hadn't blown off
the Cliffs of Moher in County Clare in 1972,
I wouldn't be sitting here poking the eyes out
of a potato if that had been the case, would I?

Try to describe grief. If only there was a day
when my daughter would not leave
that picture of herself on her father's bed
with Hi, Dad, remember me? written on it.
If only he would remember to notice,
even once, it might make a difference. But Dad's
on the nod again, smudging the Winnebago
and I'm all done with the I'm sorry's,
I only wish I could help you out of this.

Anne Boleyn was the first woman
I ever looked up to, it takes balls
to say, the executioner is, I hear, very expert
and my neck is very slender when
the hangman says, no noose is good noose,
like every anesthetist I've known who thinks
cracking bad jokes is the way to put you under.
It takes cojones the size of coconuts

to lose your head while all around you
are keeping theirs, doing the housework,
ejaculating prematurely, oh, yes, I'm coming

down hard, what is it, you ask, I love most
about my life? Is it possible to be
honest? Behaviour doesn't just happen, you say,
there are always underlying causes. But who
can handle it? In "Applying Biblical Truth"
I read it is helpful to see people as having
some of the characteristics of icebergs,
and that "Christians are like a tea-bag."
Shouldn't it be "Christians are like tea-bags"?

Metaphor frightens me. Last night
at my Al-Anon meeting one woman talked
about moving the large rocks off her vacant lot
and getting up in the morning to see
a whole bunch of smaller rocks she hadn't
noticed before because the larger rocks
were in the way, and I was the only person
in the room who didn't know the rocks
were supposed to be problems. I mean
I was thinking, why didn't she just hire
a fucking bulldozer to get rid of all the rocks
at once, but everyone else was nodding
like they knew rocks stood for something
that stands in our way. I could never be
a heroin addict because I can't stand
doing the same thing day after day.
Grief is the price we pay

for love, you say, but as of today
I'm all out of love, and its subsidiaries.
Behaviour doesn't just happen but I can't handle it
when it does. Two years in maximum security
is the price my mother paid for trailing Knowlton
and his bedroom eyes all the way to Africa.

Try to describe sorrow. When I found
my lover's new sunglasses face-down
in the gravel, the lenses smashed out, two
half-eaten Snickers bars blocking the toilet,
a wallet greasy with money, I felt sad at last,
I felt everything was over. Wrong again,
it was only a new beginning. But
every time I find another C-note on the floor
I make a contribution to the Kill for Peace
in Kosovo Organization, which is how I won
the Nobel Prize, by saving all the proceeds
of a slipping-down life I found scattered
around the house, enough to make Milošević come
to his senses: I took him to my carnal garage
and gave him a chance to experience what
Canadian women are famous for. After that he said
war wasn't doing it for him anymore, killing
wasn't giving him what he needed. The day I won

the Nobel Prize for Peace I blew up
in front of the television. I couldn't take it
anymore, my mother being front-page news
also, and everybody looking for answers

as if by stopping the war in Kosovo
I should have been able to stop
my mother. Later I made a statement
about the aging inmate population in America,
more prisoners dying of heart attacks than from
lethal injection/electric chair/gas chamber/firing squad
put together. Try to describe a fist a split
second before it hits your lip, or the way
a syringe sucks up blood, or the quiet death
a person sometimes comes to: what happens
to plum blossom after spring snow?
Try to describe love – what other word
might there have been for it? I know now there is
no greater loneliness than in its brief shining.

LOVE'S TOURMALINE SHIRT STUDS

How could I know when I came to the inter-
section of Heaven and Highway 7
that a driver wearing nothing
but green-black pyjama bottoms would pull out
in front of me in a black Cadillac

convertible with the top open. I signalled
to turn right at the 7-Eleven south of the inter-
section of Highway 7 and Heaven; I signalled
but then this voice from the wilder days cried,
hey baby, let me buy you a last syringe,
his bloodshot eyes going to bed with my bones
on that lonely Ontario hardtop.

We were sniffing the bee balm then,
doing the bebop on that cracked black-
top when the sirens came on
and this voice said, *hey baby, they're playing
our song.* I saw myself burning

out across the inter-
section of Heaven and Highway 7
and I remember thinking the clouds
looked like ambulance attendants
floating over me wearing green-black
pyjama bottoms, blacker than grief
on television, greener than my love's
tourmaline shirt studs.

So it is when you dream
your soul in flight, the angels
becoming attendants in green cowboy shirts
unbuttoned to show the hurting black
hair on their bodies. The driver
has sped off up Heaven toward the 7-Eleven
you know now you won't ever reach, not
in this life, maybe never. Not even the kids
kicking dust on the corner saw him go,
not one witness on the eleven o'clock television.
Nobody remembers the stoplights
going out, one by one, all over the world

or the driver, greener than a hangover
in his talk-show coffin, blacker
than the scars on a serial killer's conscience

cruising through the intersection strewn
with smoking bodies, drunk and careening
over the white lines of the bloodied
PED-XING, chanting, *burn baby burn* in flame-
retardant green-black pyjama bottoms.

  (a last gift from Al Purdy, his way
  of saying he considered me to be
  a bona fide poet(ess))

By the time I reach the Sumerians
I have grown weary of our suffering,
we who have stood on tiptoe gazing
across eons, while the mole-cricket
makes a doleful chirping on the wind.
My own sorrows being many, I feel
for the second wife whose aching body
is deemed unworthy, who cries about
the house sniffing a rare piece of cloth
her Imperial Master left her when he sailed
upriver to do business in the capital.

I want to say, buck up, act like a man.
You heard he was unfaithful? Get your hands
on his cash, sell the crib and the ride,
donate the rest to charity, but they –
these women from antiquity –
won't hear me, ten thousand clouds
and a Tartar wind stand in their way.

What can I give my absent man? is their
age-old lament and if you wade through enough
mist and over an eternity of mountain
passes, after 600 pages you'll find an answer:
death. From now on every poem has a corpse

served up in it, the way we seem to prefer
our men – half-devoured, floating
on cloud omelettes, and laying off
our bodies at last. But then

the suicide poems begin, the ones
that end *if he telephones again tell him
not to keep trying* and I think, ladies,
we're doing it again, suffocating our bodies
in death silk as we go about suffering.
We ache, gain weight, and yearn for that
fearful day when fresh love shows up and we
can crush it to death before it dies
of natural causes. I skip through more

centuries until I reach the present
day and discover it is women we now desire
most, six-armed goddesses who smell of heat
and same-sex grief, those recreated in our own
images, ourselves at last. Sappho's mother
claimed she stayed eternally in fashion
wearing purple ribbons in her hair
and not much has changed, heartache
will always be fashionable in poetry, the way
torture has become *haute couture* because
it objectifies the body. For years we prayed
to a God who ordered us to drink his tears
and vowed we would not die for our weeping.
We prayed to a God who lied. Sisters,
that was then. Not now. Ah, men.

MY STUDENTS DARE ME TO WRITE A HAPPY POEM
INCORPORATING THE WORD *BOSOM*,
AND ON TWO COUNTS, AT LEAST, I FAIL

> There is never any healing. Ever. When a wound "heals" it leaves a
> permanent scar . . .
> – George Carlin

The poem I have not allowed myself to write
is the happy poem, the one where all the catastrophes
I have spent my life suffering
never happen, like the dream where my breasts
break free of their restraints and pop up again
in front of a train on the newly established
Rocky Mountaineer Fraser Discovery Route,
where the driver, who "never saw them coming,"
develops a phobia about airbags and is caught
puncturing hot-air balloons at a Canada Day
parade. The happy poem is one where my ex-better
half Bob does not run away with that mud-bogger
he met at AA, the "guy" with the pierced nipples.
The poem I have not allowed myself to write
is the one where ex-Bob never
finds out I told my writing class he goes to AA
because "at least he can get an effing cup
of coffee there." Ex-Bob tells his ex-
drinking group I wouldn't know what to do
with a coffee pot if he hit me over the head
with one. The happy poem is the poem where
my ex-best friend doesn't cook and eat her lover,
then go on TV to explain how she did it
to spice up her common-law relationship

before spontaneously exposing her weapons
of mass distraction on *Larry King Live*. The happy
poem is the one where ex-Bob does not find out
I wrote a poem about him quitting AA
the same day he told me he had always preferred
my ex-friend's ham curtains to my own –
there are some things you can't take back once
you've stated them, ham curtains being a bodacious
example. The poem I have not allowed myself to write

is the one where I start to obsess about worse-case
scenarios, my brain over-percolating like the aluminium
coffee pot with the dent in it Bob made hitting me
back when we still loved each other enough
to want to kill each other on a daily basis.
The happy poem does not include the stick
drawings my daughter makes of her perfect body
lacking only a full complement of limbs.
My therapist says this means she has difficulty
expressing her feelings and cuts herself
off, symbolically speaking, instead. Ex-Bob thinks
self-harm reduction is the menu of the day, he who
drinks surreptitiously and crash-bangs the family car
when he isn't up in his ivory soap tower where he
sequestered himself the day I confessed I had gone
from a 42C to a 36B on account of a cosmetic bust
reduction offered on sale at Walmart. Ex-Bob
used to brag I had floaters the size of the inflatable
life rafts on the *Titanic* before she went tits up after
being punctured by a bergy bit. Until he saw my ex-
friend's silicone earmuffs on *Larry King Live* and split
with her to Amazonialand where she stars in her own
cannibal cooking show, part of her healing process.

But who am I to judge, I who abandoned
my drastically reduced Dolly Partons in a Quesnel
Walmart? The poem I have not allowed myself to write
until now sings "Release Me" in the shower, a halfway-
to-being-happy poem soaping its cut-price wounds.

FRED BIGGAR SWIMS NUDE
IN THE REFLECTING POND WITH KOI

> Poetry is an orphan of silence. The words
> never quite equal the experience behind them.
> – Charles Simic

For a week I had been telling them, rules
were made to be broken, go out and do something
irresponsible, write the poem that will change the world,
but I never expected them to take me literally. Since when
have poets ever listened to anything
but the drugging sounds of their own voices
insisting they exist? So when three of the best
set out to behave in a way that would impress
their instructor without discrediting the Optional
Residency MFA in Creative Writing Program
at UBC, their destination after an evening
at the beer garden being the Japanese Tea Garden,
most enjoyable when time is available for thought
and reflection, I was pleased. These magnificent three
renewed my faith in the ability of poets
to choose the road less travelled and find themselves

lost. "I am in Japan," insisted the Emperor
of that country the first time he visited the garden
best experienced by strolling in a counterclockwise
manner, one intended to mirror the passage
of the moon. Fred and his entourage,
unlike the Emperor, arrived after closing time,
the blind leading the visibly impaired by moonlight,

weaving straight through the orderly conifers
surrounding the garden *where equilibrium is
paramount.* Once over the wall they began to grope

their way, one which had begun with a single pale
ale and led to a zigzag bridge over a susurrus of blue
irises surrounding the turtle-shaped Island of Eternity.
In Japan it is believed that evil spirits travel
in straight lines, and cannot follow anyone
over a zigzag bridge, but after an evening of spirited
libations the zigzag bridge seemed straight enough
to Fred who had paused to watch the Jesus bugs
play hopscotch over the lily pads in the reflecting pond
when a school of white koi tinged with gold rose up,
a sign, Fred interpreted, for him to cast off
his clothing and join them.

What the koi thought of Fred, an Emperor
with no clothes, only the Jesus bugs know,
but Adrienne says she will never forget the sight
of him creeping naked from campus security,
through the rushes, as an evening mist
might have crept, because he was a teacher
of English with a reputation to protect. "We're poets
on an assignment," Adrienne told security,
"and we're supposed to change the world." With this
the guards unholstered their tasers, and the one
with the slim volume of unpublishable odes in his eyes
said, *quote us a poem, then, to prove you are certifiable.* Tadzio
rose to the occasion and recited the ghazal he'd composed
about going mad and fucking on a sink in a university
bathroom down the hall from the religious studies
department and later against a car in a parking

garage with a nun, how he has a bad habit
of following random lusts so came here to meditate
on the stone Buddha's head for spiritual release
instead. While the guards argued about line
breaks and whether form is expressive of content,
Fred made a clean getaway back over the bamboo wall
into the conifers where he clothed himself
in darkness, humbled that something so small
and ordinary as a random act of poetry
extends our lives.

Smuggle them to Paris and fling them
into the Seine. P.S. He was wrong
when he wrote, "To Paris Never Again"

Put them in an egg-timer – that way
he can go on being useful, at least
for three minutes at a time
(pulverize him first, in a blender)

Like his no good '48 Pontiac
refusing to turn over in below-zero weather,
let the wreckers haul his ashes away

Or stash them in the trunk of your car:
when you're stuck in deep snow sprinkle them
under your bald tires for traction

Mix them with twenty tonnes of concrete,
like Lawrence at Taos, erect
a permanent monument to his banned
poetry in Fenelon Falls

Shout, "these ashes oughta be worth some beer!"
in the tavern at the Quinte Hotel, and wait
for a bottomless glass with yellow flowers in it
to appear

Mix one part ashes to three parts
homemade beer in a crock under the table,
stir with a broom, and consume
in excessive moderation

Fertilize the dwarf trees at the Arctic Circle
so that one day they might grow to be
as tall as he, always the first
to know when it was raining

Scatter them at Roblin's Mills
to shimmer among the pollen
or out over Roblin Lake
where the great boing they make
will arouse summer cottagers

Place them beside your bed where they can
watch you make love, vulgarly
and immensely, in the little time left

Declare them an aphrodisiac, more potent
than the gallbladder of a bear
with none of the side effects of Viagra

Stitch them in the hem of your summer dress
where his weight will keep it
from flying up in the wind, exposing
everything: he would like that

Let them harden, the way the heart must harden
as the might lessens, then lob them
at the slimy, drivelling, snivelling,
palsied, pulseless lot of critics who ever uttered
a single derogatory phrase in anti-praise
of his poetry

Award them the Nobel Prize
for humility

Administer them as a dietary supplement
to existential Eskimo dogs with a preference
for violet toilet paper and violent
appetites for human excrement: dogs
that made him pray daily
for constipation in Pangnirtung

Bequeath them to Margaret Atwood,
casually inserted between the covers
of Wm Barrett's Irrational Man

Lose them where the ghosts of his Cariboo
horses graze on, when you stop to buy oranges
from the corner grocer at 100 Mile House

Distribute them from a hang-glider
over the Galápagos Islands
where blue-footed boobies will shield him
from over-exposure to ultraviolet rays

Offer them as a tip to the shoeshine boys
on the Avenida Juárez, all twenty of them
who once shined his shoes for one peso
and twenty centavos – nine and a half cents –
years ago when nine and a half cents
was worth twice that amount

Encapsulate them in the ruins of Quintana Roo
under the green eyes of quetzals, Tulum parrots,
and the blue, unappeasable sky –
that 600 years later they may still be warm

Declare them culturally modified property
and have them preserved for posterity
in the Museum of Modern Man and, as
he would be the first to add, Modern Wife

As a last resort auction them off
to the highest bidder, the archives
at Queens or Cornell where
Auden's tarry lungs wheeze on
next to the decomposed kidneys of Dylan Thomas;
this will ensure Al's survival in Academia, also

But on no account cast his ashes to the wind:
they will blow back in your face as if to say
he is, in some form, poetic or other, here
to stay, with sestinas still to write
and articles to rewrite
for The Imperial Oil Review

No, give these mortal remains away
that they be used as a mojo to end the dirty
cleansing in Kosovo, taken as a cure
for depression in Namu, B.C., for defeat
in the country north of Belleville, for poverty
hopping a boxcar west out of Winnipeg
all the way to Vancouver, for heroin addiction
in Vancouver; a cure for loneliness
in North Saanich, for love in Oaxaca,
courtship in Cuernavaca, adultery
in Ameliasburgh, the one sure cure
for extremely deep hopelessness
in the Eternal City, for death, everywhere,
pressed in a letter sent whispering to you.

PART FOUR

HEROINES

This guy says to me, I know this place
like the back of my hand, I'll show you
around, only his hand has been lopped
off at the wrist and we end up getting lost
in this junkie neighbourhood and I says,
thanks for the memories but I'm outta here.

I wasn't going to turn out like my friend
who wrote NOTHING every day in her diary
because that was the only word
she remembered how to spell: I am
nothing, I will be nothing, I always was
nothing – she learned a few other words
too, but in the end only NOTHING stuck.

I didn't intend to end up like that.
I knew I had a lot more going for me.

That first week in town I bought
a T-shirt: LIFE'S A BEACH

but I never made it as far as any beach
around here, I had a full-time job
just getting out of bed in the morning
and trying to find someone who had
ten bucks so I could get high.

Sometimes I'd think, fuck
living like this but I never got past
the corner before I'd have to turn back
trying to return to that state
of grace I once had before
every one of my veins collapsed
until the only usable blood vessel
in my body was under my tongue.

Heroin. Her-row-in. Whatever way
you cut it, nobody understands
what it means the way I do.

PICTURE-MAN

(i)

You're beautiful, he says
he wants to take
a picture of me

but I'm getting sick
and my shoes are killing me
and I'm sweating in my
long sleeves – I figured
the track marks wouldn't turn out
all that brilliant in living colour.

He's not into colour
he says, I can roll up my
sleeves. So how do I look
in black and white, I says,
still like what you see?

He wants a profile –
tells me to turn my head
one way, then the other:
what's my good side? I say

The inside, he says to me.

(ii)

I wanted him to make me look
like what I dreamed of being –
a runway model – the kind of look
that makes a man want to start laying down
big money, and my legs long enough
to stretch all the way to Paris
or somewhere else important.

Where was I?

I wanted women to stare at me
not because they pitied or hated me.

(iii)

This could be a photograph
of me. It's snowing: it is
me? I must have been sick then,
I needed ten bucks to get better

I remember you offered me five
just to take my picture
just to be *me* only now
it doesn't look like me.

Look at her, she's got
blood on her face
she had a fight that day

When is she ever going to
get rid of those crutches?

I was in Detox with this girl
she's pretty here but she
ruined her face. She never
loved herself, that's
what they'd probably say.

This is my best friend – was –
we were in jail together
she's missing
I don't know if I can say
she is my best friend
when she's missing

I do know there's a whole lot more
to being missing than it
sounds like in one word

All these girls, they're pretty,
they have the heroin look.
You can see them thinking,
the hustle's on how am I going
to get my fix down when am I going
to come up with ten dollars or even nine

In these pictures I can tell you
every last one of them
is thinking the same thing

where am I going to get my next fix
I have to get straightened out here
and after that's out of the way
I can get started on my day.

(iv)

A photograph is a secret
about a secret, he says,
the more it tells you the less
you see. So what does this picture
say about me?

(v)

Lonely eyes, hungry eyes, vacant eyes
lying eyes, crying eyes, flirting eyes
bedroom eyes, faraway eyes, dark eyes
hollow eyes, hurting blue eyes
fucky brown eyes, yellow eyes
cat's eyes, black eyes, black-and-blue
eyes, baby blue eyes, startled eyes
leave me alone eyes, sad night eyes

eyes caught in the headlights of a speeding
car, fumbling with a zipper eyes, round
eyes, keep your eyes to yourself
keep your eyes open, the whites
of your eyes, eyes for no one but you
use your eyes, open your eyes, close your eyes
an eye for an eye, they rape us
with their eyes in the wink of an eye

smiling eyes distant eyes blind eyes
heroin honeymoon eyes, dope-sick eyes

how little our eyes
let us see

You don't find it around here, love
checked out hours ago with her works
as if this hospital they call Mercy
were some downtown hotel where you come
and pay for your room by the hour. It's not like
she ever wanted me, and my father never did

and when you're not wanted that way
from the beginning it keeps
raining inside you forever.

What's most missing in my life is love
but I'm only good for one thing
that's all I know, and love's got nothing
to do with it. Still friends
he asked, after he burned my hair
and threw my clothes into the street
so I would always have to remember
what it felt like to have nothing.

you've got this mother and she's
pregnant with you but it gets
fucked up and she has this
abortion and you spend
the rest of your life just
mopping up. Mopping up
someone else's mess
that turns out to be you. Mopping up
the blood off the worn-out lino
your mother spent every day waxing,
for what?

Blood off the black-eyed Susans
your father sent when it didn't work out

Blood off your lips
when he kissed you goodbye for good

Blood you smeared across
a piece of white bread then fed
to your baby daughter
crying, Feed me I'm sick.
She choked to death and there was blood
on your hands afterwards

only you refused to feel much
because – what were you supposed to feel?

Feelings? Don't talk to me about
feelings, I thought God

would let me keep the one thing I loved,
the small piece of heaven that
popped out of me like a tiny shiny
lifesaver; if I prayed
like a motherfucker I thought
he would let her live.

See what I mean? I fucked up
big-time believing for a moment
in a God like that. He's a guy, right,
and when the next guy stopped to pick me up
I've had it up to here, I said,
take me where there is everything.
I was bent over a toilet throwing up
the rest of the night, my ribcage
kicked open, my guts hanging out.

It's like that with men.
They don't take no for an answer.

QUESTION:

Did you have any dreams?
What did you want to be?

What I wanted to be? There's a
question. I was a cover girl
once, a fashion model; for a while
I thought I'd died and gone to my next life,
but then I got high, started losing
weight, I got too skinny for what they wanted
me to be. The last shots they took
I'm wearing gloves up to my elbows
to hide the tracks. White gloves,
soft as cotton balls, but I don't mind
the change, the fast life
goes by even quicker around here.

The runway, the alleyway, it's all
the same. Sex, drugs, money – the same.
It's got the same look, the same hook,
the same old same. For a while after I quit
selling my body I felt like I was living
on borrowed time and anything I couldn't borrow
I would steal. Anything to get high. To stay
high. I wanted to eat this mother up, suck
every last bit of marrow from the bone of life.

QUESTION:

What do you think about
when you're having sex?

I promise him I'll do anything
if that's what he wants to hear

but mostly under all that promising
I'm not really there

I'm a kid again, diving down
deep to retrieve a coin
of any description. The men
always let us keep what we
came up with; I was the best
because I could stay under
the longest, coming up for air
only because I had to.

I promised myself a better life.
I had earned it.

QUESTION:

How do you feel about men?

One day I'd like to meet a guy
who'd get out of the car and open
the door for me, not just wait for me
to climb in off the curb because
he knows I'm sick and he can get me
to do anything for ten bucks so
I can start feeling better. I'd like to
meet a guy who'd buy me flowers; I don't
belong down here but I guess no one does.
To love someone like me you'd have to be
already filled up with emptiness. I arrived
here with just the clothes on my back
and that's the way I'll leave.

QUESTION:

Have you been hurt by men,
have you been raped?

I've been raped, yes,
but what hurts worse is the way
they look at you afterwards
when they refuse to pay

as if you're the one dirty habit
they can't break.

QUESTION:

What do they think about you,
the people who pass you on the street?
What would you like them to see?

They see the druggie, the whore, the junkie.
I'd like them to see me as their daughter,
a sister, a lover, their mother.

They see garbage, blood, feces.
They see us in alleyways passed out in heaps,
sick, crazy for a fix.

I'd like them to see me as a dancer
who can't remember the steps, a singer
whose voice has left her, a woman whose heart
has grown as empty as every naked hotel room
she's ever tried to check out of.

They see needles, spoons, condoms,
think HIV, AIDS. I want them to think
how hard I try to live.

When they cruise the street,
stop for a red light at the corner
where I stand waiting in the rain

they see scabs on my face, festering
sores, scars, rotting teeth.

When they rev their engines, crank
up the heat, I want them to see how the only
desire left in me is the desire
to make the best of it.

QUESTION:

What is it like to be homeless,
to live on the street?

He's got a big heart,
picture-man, he gave me
an address book.

My own address book!

I couldn't stop
laughing about having
a real live actual
address book

until I thought about it

If I had a choice I wouldn't be
a heroin addict; I'd get up each day
and do something different.
I'd be a mother to my daughter,
that would be enough for me.

I wanted to be a teacher, or an actress
but most of all a mother. I didn't want to be
a heroin addict, I said I would never
stick needles in my arms or let any man
make a bitch out of me. My goal was to be
a good mother, not like the mothers I had.

I'd want my daughter to speak her feelings,
say them out loud. I'd teach her to cry
but only if she wanted to. Heroin
doesn't let you do that. It hurts for you.

It thinks for you, it lives for you,
it fucks for you. It has no passion
except for you. It has no God but you.

It takes up in you, pushing you down
making you small. And when you're so small,
no bigger than the light from a match someone
strikes in the dark, the person you love
most could strike a match on your soul
and it wouldn't make you flinch.

I never named the baby when he was born
I was pretty sure he wasn't going to make it

for a while I even joked about him being born
with a bent spoon in his mouth

but I guess it wasn't that funny
to most people and it wasn't funny
to me, I just couldn't cry about it
for too long because I mean, hey
girl, get over it, know what I mean?

I kept forgetting his birthday
that's why I got this tattoo,
I wanted something permanent.
And the day he died, I forgot that, too.
The guy who gave me the tattoo said
not to rush into anything, death
was like falling in love
it made people do crazy shit.

So do it to me, I said, what have I got
to lose? And I chose a heart, something
I wasn't likely to have
mixed feelings about later.

"It'll hurt," he said, but after a few days
even that pain began to disappear.

I've had my share – a real one
who went to Toronto to quit drinking,
he said when he came back we'd be
a family again but he never came back.
Adopted fathers, foster fathers,
group-home fathers, and one I was sent to
to confess my sins. I grew up thinking
a man's knee was something you sat
naked on, something I should be

grateful for. I try to imagine a world
where someone is grateful for anything.

The father I hated best? The one who
paid me for sex. We lived on a farm
and if I said no to him he threatened
to kill one of my favourite pets,
some maimed creature, a runt I'd
raised myself until it grew strong enough
to fend for itself; he told me I'd be next.
I'd go with him, early, before daylight
to feed the animals and do the things
he told me to do, down on my knees.

Now when I'm pulling a date,
I'm not really there, I'm doing what
I wanted to do when I was growing up.
I wanted to be an animal trainer, to
train animals to run and keep running
forever, like some wild part of me
no one can ever touch.

Most of the time I played with my dolls
outside while my parents stayed inside
and fought, that's what I remember
about my childhood. If I came inside
it would be go to your room get out
of my sight but I didn't have any room
to go to, so I went inside myself. Same
thing when I was diddled, it just put me
deeper inside myself.

Afterwards I would sit in the bathtub
scrubbing my dolls, scrubbing my brown skin
to make it white. Clean and white not
brown, which meant dirty winos,
drug addicts, welfare bums. I tried
to believe I could wash myself away.
I still don't like looking at myself
in the mirror.

The difference between nothing and zero,
that's the difference my life makes
he'd say to me, each time I left the house.
What do I like about heroin? The rush,
the ringing. You're in your own little world.
That nothing can satisfy your hunger for more.

One time the man who calls himself our father
made me crawl to him on a carpet of broken
glass. There are days I feel
as old as the Bible he makes me read –

he says it's a good book, full of lessons
I have to learn, like when to bend
over our father's knee and let his fingers
enter me because I have sinned. One time
for seven days he made me lie in a grave
with the dog I let out of the yard next door;
he got run over by the man who beat him
every day – I'd just wanted to help that dog
get away. Our father said I should pray
and I do but it don't change much of anything.
The dog never gets his life back no matter
how long I lie there, naked and ashamed
of myself, beside him.

I remember the sound of the skin being sliced
from my body, of glass cutting bone. Even when
he entered me I wasn't allowed to cry,
crying was for babies not girls like me.
I tore, but I wouldn't bleed. Over and over
again I was torn but I wouldn't bleed,
and I don't think he ever forgave me
for holding out on him.

After he had me there would be blood
on the bedspread, all over the sheets,
I got so used to it I didn't think
you could have sex without blood, the two
went together, like grief and laughter
they had a joined-at-the-hip relationship,
the kind I had with the rooster my foster-dad
kept tied by one leg to the bedpost in the
spare room where I slept. It was called
the spare room even though it had been
my room ever since I had come to live
with them on the farm, spare as in extra,
spare as in not very much. The rooster got less
than I did, a dish of water he shit in
as if to let them know what he thought
of the treatment he got. A few seeds,
hardly enough, he scattered all over the
rug; I learned not to ask how's he supposed
to eat with his beak tied shut. My father would
only say spare me the grief.

The rooster had flown at him once,
ripping his face, then tearing around
the yard like a chicken with his head cut off
(my foster mother said) and spitting out
my father's tough lips by the pig trough.
Killing him would be too quick, my father said,
there were worse things than death,
and so he, too, was spared
and made to live.

I had one married guy who kept coming
back for me, he called me doll-face
because in those days I always lugged
a headless doll around with me
one I found in a dumpster and thought
that's a pretty sad place for any doll
to end up, even if a big piece
of her has gone missing. Doll-face,

that's a joke

You don't get it? Neither did he.

BAD DATE

The whole time I never stop
looking him in the eye, he wants me
to cry or beg but I won't give him
the satisfaction. I just fix
onto his eyes, all the time working
to get my hands free; duct tape is like
everything – it's got a lifespan.
He rapes me, sticks a gun down my throat,
and sodomizes me, but nothing he does
gets a rise out of me. Not until he burns me,
flicking matches onto my skin where they stick
and I smell my own flesh burning
do I break: I sweat, I start to shake,
and then a tear I can't stop slips down
my face – just one – that's all
it takes, he knows I am his.

He's given me a taste, am I ready
to eat? I tell him if I'm hungry
I'll eat, there's nothing
that doesn't belong to me.

It's not something you go looking for
like a woman on her knees
searching for something invisible
in a carpet so threadbare
it looks as if it has been laid
upside down. It's not like it

keeps you awake all night
when the pipes are frozen and
the only thing moving in the room
is the picture on the TV where a gentleman
found guilty of raping another prostitute
is saying to the judge, "You got to be
kidding, right?" when the judge tells him
he is throwing away the key.

I had a key once, to a heart-shaped
locket I kept locked so tight I thought
no one would ever break
into it. I would never let anyone
get close enough to try, because I kept
a piece of my baby's heart inside
and a Welcome to the World card that said
You Go, Girl!!! I named her Grace
as in Grace of God because
she kept me alive. You don't go
looking for love if you want to survive.

"I'm not kidding either," the woman
on the rug says to the judge on TV,

"throw away the key," then because
she sees me staring at how thin
she has become, says, "I used to be fat.
"Men could do anything
they wanted to me. They thought
I'd be grateful." She has to stop and
light a cigarette, and suck it hard.
"And I was – grateful. It's like when
you're sad and you cry. Any man
will fuck you when your mascara's
all over your face."

The only thing I ever wanted
was to be held, it's what we all want.
Is that asking too much?

Come here, baby girl, he says to me,
like he wants to help me find
a part of me that is missing.
Love's hard to find when you're
fourteen in your mother's baby
dolls with red hearts all over them
and your father's pushing downwards
on the back of your head.

But some nights you find love
in the cold blue-steel grip
of a razor blade that's way
past caring. You carve
LOVE in the vein on your
right arm, HATE in the left,
but the blood runs into the same pool
at your feet, no longer a thin line even

between love and hate. Rape happens
when you work on the street
you know you deserve better
and you're waiting for it.

You mean to live.
You mean it.
Hurt me, baby girl, he says.
Use your fists.

I got off the plane in my jailhouse
clothes, kicked back, and before
I knew it I was shooting coke
at the Cambie Hotel wearing
long sleeves on an 80-degree day
to cover my tracks. My son, he stayed
in California with his dad.

The hardest thing I ever did? Coming here,
not knowing anyone, having to leave
my kid. I'll get him back though, as soon
as I go to Detox and get my life straightened out.
That's what I'm planning to do. Get dressed.
Kick back. Get my life back.

I wish to thank the many dedicated editors of literary magazines
and the editors of anthologies who continue to publish the writers
of this country, against all odds.

Many of these poems have appeared in the following magazines
and newspapers: The Café Review, Canadian Poetry, Cider Press Review,
Event, Grain, Literary Review of Canada, The Malahat Review, National
Post, New Delta Review, Out of Bounds, Room of One's Own, Shoreline,
subTerrain, The Cooweescoowee, Twenty-Five Years of Tree (edited by
James Moran and Jennifer Mulligan), and Lake.

ANTHOLOGIES:
The March Hare Anthology (Breakwater Books; edited by Adrian
     Fowler)
Long Journey: Contemporary Northwest Poets (Oregon State University
     Press; edited by David Biespiel)
The Echoing Years: An Anthology of Poetry from Canada and Ireland
     (edited by John Ennis, Randall Maggs, and Stephanie McKenzie)
Rocksalt (edited by Harold Rhenisch and Mona Fertig)

ONLINE PUBLICATIONS:
CBC News Online first published "Origami Dove" in 1999. Other
poems have been published online in forget magazine and Einstein's
Tongue.

RADIO:

The CBC commissioned "Rest Area: No Loitering, and Other Signs of the Times" for broadcast on New Year's Eve 1999.

"Friday Evening" first appeared under the title "Anny's Eggs" in *Home: Tales of a Heritage Farm*, by Anny Scoones, published by Hedgerow Press.

The poem "Thirty-Two Uses for Al Purdy's Ashes" was originally published as "Twenty-Eight Uses for Al Purdy's Ashes" in a limited-edition chapbook from the Hawthorne Society of Arts and Letters.

"Ice-Age Lingerie" won first prize in a writing contest and was published in the anthology *Panty Lines* from Blue Moon Press.

My thanks to Ursula Vaira at Leaf Press for publishing some of the poems in *Obituary of Light: The Sangan River Meditations*, in a cherished Leaf Press edition. Part (viii) in the section "Fall" is featured on Vancouver buses in the Poetry-in-Transit program. A version of "Winter (vii)" was published in *Art or War*, edited by Shirarose Wilensky of Tightrope Books.

The poems in the sequence *Heroines* were drawn from the life stories of six women, heroin-addicted prostitutes, from Vancouver's Downtown Eastside. Director Stan Feingold (The Eyes Multimedia Productions) commissioned me to write a "script" for a one-hour documentary art film – a series of original poems. Segments of these poems were used as voiceover in *Heroines*, which premiered on Bravo! on Father's Day 2001 and launched the fall 2002 season of the CBC's *Rough Cuts*.

Heroines follows photographer Lincoln Clarkes ("picture-man" is what the women call him) as he ventures into heroin hell – not to shoot up but to shoot portraits. My job was to find a voice in which to speak of these women's lives, from the inside out – the wrecked childhoods, addictions, the loss of their own children, their bad dates, and their dreams.

Heroines has won many awards, both at home and internationally. In 2002 it won four Golden Sheaf Awards at the Yorkton Short Film & Video Festival, the longest-running film festival in North America. In addition it was nominated for Best Editing, Best Script, and Best Director. As well, Heroines was awarded the National Film Board's Kathleen Shannon Award, which is presented to an independent filmmaker whose production "provides an opportunity for people outside the dominant culture to speak for themselves." Stan Feingold donated his prize money to a charity that works for the benefit of the women of Vancouver's Downtown Eastside, to whom this sequence is dedicated.

The sequence Heroines was published as Mother's Day Behind the West Hotel in a limited-edition chapbook from Poetgoat Press. A number of the poems were published in Walk Myself Home: An Anthology to End Violence Against Women, edited by Andrea Routley and published by Caitlin Press in 2010.